The American Flag

Learning to Identify Two-Digit Numbers Up to 50

Robert Girard

Rosen Classroom Books & Materials
New York

The American flag stands for the United States of America. You can see the flag flying in many places across America.

The American flag has stars and stripes on it.

It is red, white, and blue.

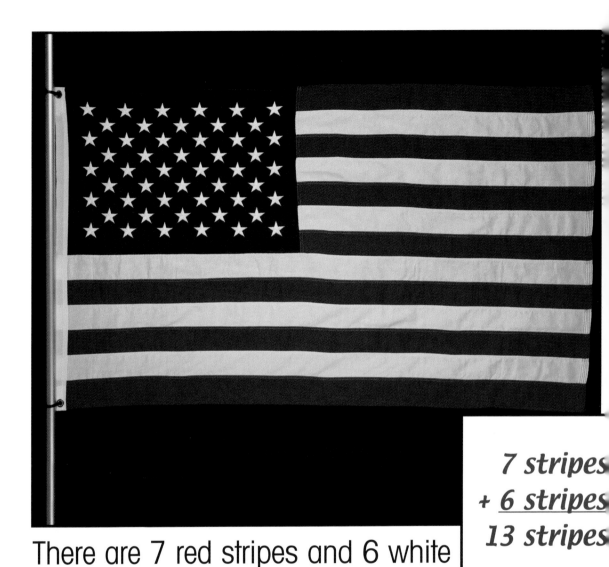

7 stripes
+ 6 stripes
13 stripes

There are 7 red stripes and 6 white stripes on the American flag. Each stripe stands for one of the nation's first states. How many stripes are there?

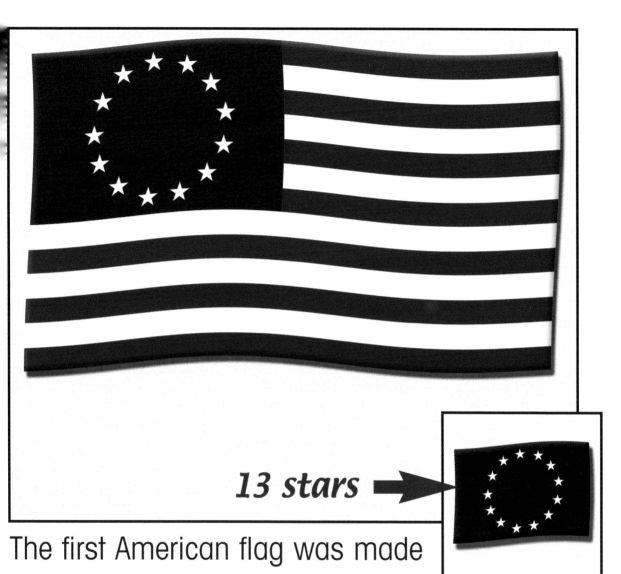

13 stars ➡

The first American flag was made around 1776. The 13 stars on this flag stand for the first 13 states in America.

5

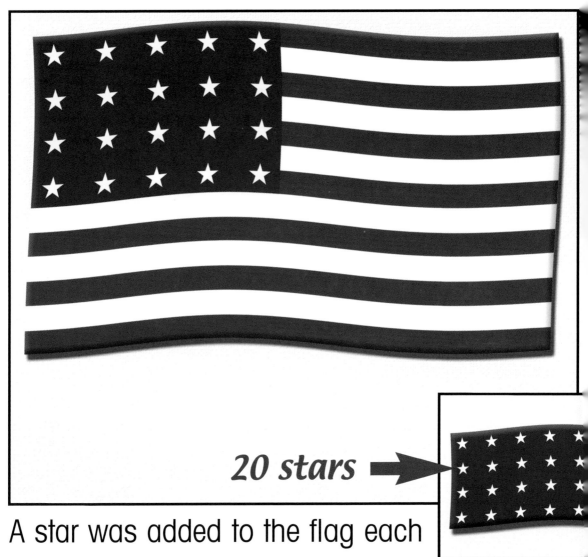

20 stars ➡

A star was added to the flag each time a new state became part of America. How many stars are on this flag?

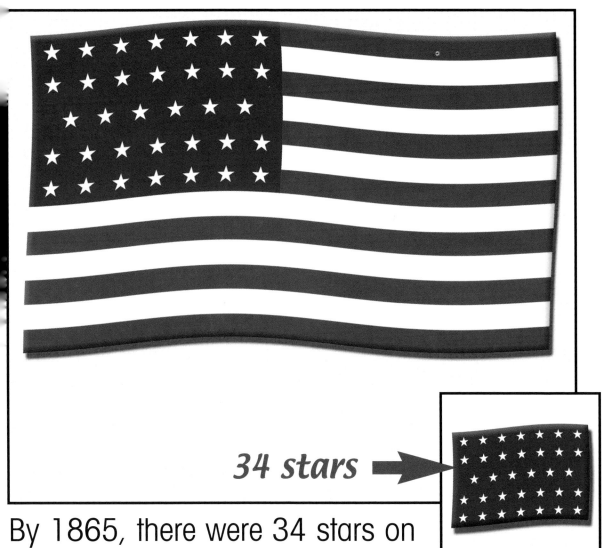

34 stars

By 1865, there were 34 stars on the flag. How many states were part of America in 1865?

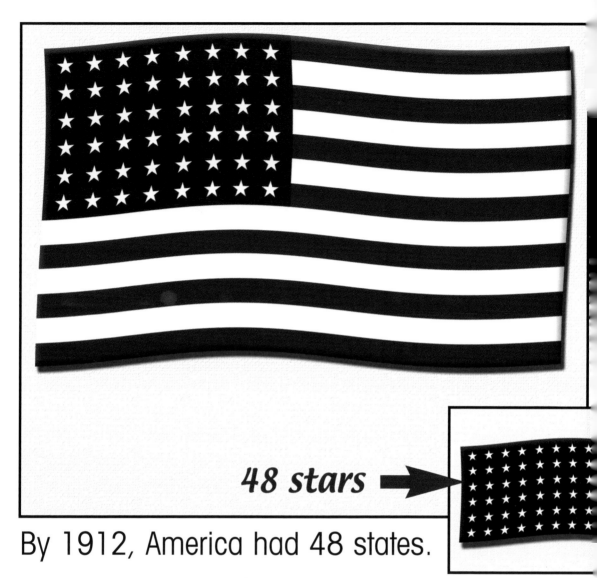

48 stars ➡️

By 1912, America had 48 states.

There were now 48 stars on the flag.

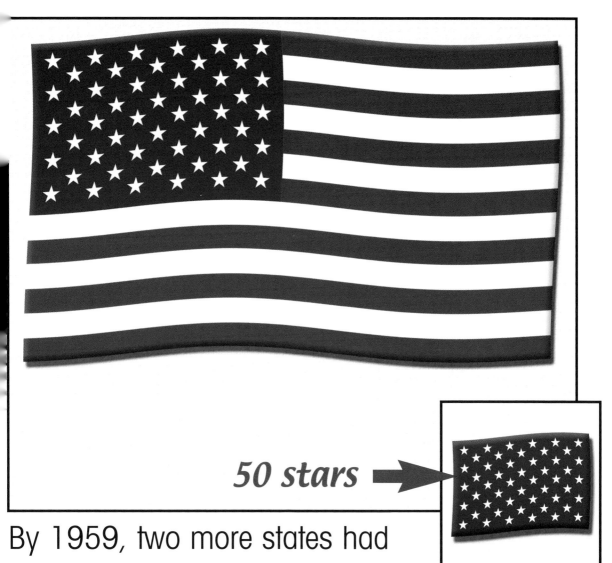

50 stars ➡️

By 1959, two more states had become part of America. This is how the American flag looks today. Now there are 50 states and 50 stars.

9

Canada

Mexico

Canada

United States of America

Mexico

All countries have their own flags. Here are the flags for Canada and Mexico, the two countries closest to America.

How many American flags do you see? How are they the same?

Words to Know

blue

flag

red

stars

stripes

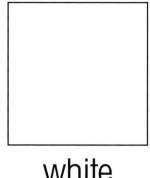

white